DATE DUE			
SEP 23			
SEP 27 1991			
FEB 17			
APR 14			
APR 10			

No. 370G Waverly Publishing Co.

Looking at BASIC

BY PENNY HOLLAND

AN EASY-READ COMPUTER ACTIVITY BOOK

Franklin Watts

New York   London   Toronto   Sydney

1985

```
10 FOR CHRIS = 1 to 10
15 PRINT "LOVE FROM MOM"
20 NEXT CHRIS
```

Photographs courtesy of: I. David Blumer: p. 10; IBM: p. 14.

R.L. 2.7 Spache Revised Formula

Just as you are different from your friends, computers are different, too. Each brand has its own special keyboard. Sometimes the keys have different names. For instance, all computers have an important key which some computers call RETURN, others call ENTER, and still others label with an arrow.

If you discover any keys or commands which are different from the ones this book names, then keep track of your changes on a special piece of paper. That way you will know what to do next time you use BASIC.

Library of Congress Cataloging in Publication Data

Holland, Penny
Looking at BASIC.

(An easy-read computer activity book)
Includes index.
Summary: An introduction to computer programming using BASIC including easy-to-follow instructions for a variety of projects.
1. Basic (Computer program language)—Juvenile literature. [Basic (Computer program language)
2. Programming (Computers) 3. Programming languages (Computers)] I. Title. II. Title: Looking at BASIC.
III. Series.
QA76.73.B3H64 1985   001.64'24   84-13834
ISBN 0-531-04893-4

Text copyright © 1985 by Penny Holland
Illustrations copyright © 1985 by Franklin Watts, Inc.
All rights reserved
Printed in the United States of America
6 5 4 3 2 1

Contents

The BASIC Language	5	A BASIC Program with Variables	20
*SOMETHING TO LEARN	6	*SOMETHING TO DO	21
Igpay Atinlay		A Penny Computer	
Using the Keyboard	6	Running the Addition Program	22
*SOMETHING TO PRACTICE	7	Adding Other Numbers	22
Meeting the Keyboard		*SOMETHING TO DO	23
A Simple BASIC Program	8	Penny Power	
*SOMETHING TO DO	9	Using Input	24
Dot To Dot		*SOME THINGS TO TRY	25
The Line Number	10	Help!	
BASIC Statements	11	Fun with BASIC	
The NEW Command	12	Round and Round with BASIC	26
Entering a BASIC Program	13	*SOMETHING TO DO	27
Running a Program	14	Penny Loops	
Listing a Program	15	Counting	28
Making Corrections	16	Experimenting with For/Next	28
*SOME THINGS TO TRY	17	Looking at BASIC	29
Printing Numbers and Strings		Find Out More About BASIC	30
Fun With Print	18	Words About Computers	31
Using a Disk Drive or Cassette	19	Index	32
Numbers and Your Computer	19		

*Indicates an activity will be found on the page

What language do you speak to your computer?

"Speak?" you ask. "Can people really talk to computers?"

Not many of today's computers can understand speech. But perhaps in the future they will. Today we "talk" to a computer through its keyboard. We type words and symbols into the keyboard to tell the computer what to do. We must give clear, step-by-step directions. These become our computer **program**.

The BASIC Language

One person speaks to another in the language they both understand. This book is written in your language—English. Could you read it if it were written in Japanese?

If you want to talk to a computer to make it obey your commands, you must use a language it understands. There are many different **programming languages**. One of the most common is called **BASIC**. The letters in the word BASIC stand for:

Beginners
All-purpose
Symbolic
Instructional
Code

BASIC is made up of some English words, some symbols, and some rules. Have you ever used a secret code to send a message to a friend? Writing a program in BASIC is like using a code to send messages to your computer.

Something to Learn

IGPAY ATINLAY: Pig Latin is a language that is fun and easy to learn. It has only two rules:

1. Take the first sound in a word and put it at the end of the word.
2. Add *ay*—the sound of long *A*.

Here are some words turned into Pig Latin:

Dog   = ogDay
House   = ouseHay
Clock   = ockClay
Window = indowWay

owNay anCay ouYay eakSPay igPay atinLay? actice-PRay! Try speaking Pig Latin's "secret code" with a friend.

Using the Keyboard

When you want to enter a BASIC program into your computer, you use the computer's keyboard. It is like typing. First you need to learn how the keys work. There are many typing books and computer programs which can help you learn to type.

Something to Practice

MEETING THE KEYBOARD: First get permission to use the computer. Have someone show you how the keyboard works. Learn the difference between typing letters and numbers. Find out what the **CURSOR** is, and see how it moves on the screen. Learn to use the **CURSOR-MOVING** keys as well as the **SPACE BAR, SHIFT,** and **RETURN** keys. Some of these keys may be named differently on your computer. Find out what yours are called. If your computer has other special keys, practice using them, too.

A Simple BASIC Program

Here is a short program written in the BASIC language:

```
10 PRINT
20 PRINT "THIS IS"
30 PRINT "MY FIRST"
40 PRINT "COMPUTER PROGRAM"
50 END
```

This program is five lines long. Can you see that each line contains a **line number**? There are also four **PRINT** **statements** and an **END statement**. Soon you will enter this program in your computer. But first let's take a closer look at its parts.

Something to Do

DOT TO DOT: To understand how a computer follows line numbers, try making DOT TO DOT puzzles for a friend. Get a pencil and paper. Draw three dots on the paper and number them. Have your friend connect the dots in order. Did your friend get a triangle? If not, try again.

Now start with a new sheet of paper. You want your friend to draw a circle, but you can make only four dots. Where would you place them? Draw the dots and number them by tens. Does your puzzle look like this?

Try it on your friend, but don't say what it is supposed to be. Chances are, your friend's picture will look more like a square than a circle. Your puzzle needs more dots. Draw a new puzzle like the last one, but this time add four more dots—one in between each of the other two. Number these new dots 15, 25, 35, and 45. Your puzzle should now look something like this.

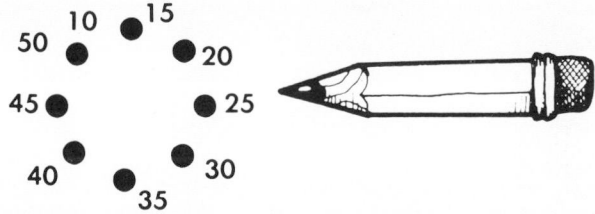

Have your friend try the new puzzle. Did the drawing come out more like a circle? For a better circle, make a puzzle with even more dots.

Now let your friend think of a shape and make a DOT TO DOT puzzle for you. If your first picture does not look quite right, your friend can add dots in between to help you.

```
LOAD NUMBER GUESSING PROGRAM
]LIST

 5 PRINT "I'M THINKING OF A NUMBER"
10 PRINT "BETWEEN 1 AND 100"
15 PRINT : PRINT "TRY TO GUESS IT!"
20 LET R = 1 + INT (RND(1) * 100)
25 INPUT G
30 IF G > R THEN PRINT "LOWER" : GOTO 25
40 IF G < R THEN PRINT "HIGHER" : GOTO 25
50 PRINT "YOU GUESSED IT!"
60 PRINT "DO YOU WANT TO PLAY AGAIN? (Y OR N)
65 INPUT A$
70 IF A$ = "Y" GOTO 5
80 END
]
```

The Line Number

In DOT TO DOT puzzles, dots are numbered in order. You connect the lowest numbered dot to the next higher one to get a picture. Like a DOT TO DOT puzzle, each line in a BASIC program begins with a **line number**. Line numbers tell the computer what order to do the steps in. Even if program lines are mixed up, the computer finds the smallest line number and does that step first. Then it finds the next larger number, the next, and so on.

Remember how you added more dots to the circle puzzle? If your dots had been numbered 1, 2, 3, and 4, you could not have fit more dots between. For the same reason, computer programmers often number their program lines by fives or tens. Later they can add steps in between if they need to fix a program. Notice that the lines are numbered 10, 20, 30, 40, and 50 in our BASIC program above.

BASIC Statements

Special words, called **statements**, are used in BASIC programs. They tell the computer to do something. The computer knows, for instance, that **END** means to stop the program. If you said FINISH, the computer would not understand. FINISH is not a BASIC word. Using an END statement is a *must* on some computers. Even if END is not necessary on your computer, it is good to get into the habit of using it.

In the last program, the words following **PRINT** are *not* BASIC words the computer understands. That is why we put **quotation marks** around them. Quotation marks are symbols that look like this " ". They tell the computer to print on the screen whatever is between them. When there is nothing after PRINT, then the computer leaves a blank line on the screen.

The *New* Command

How do you like eating dessert on an unwashed dinner plate? Does chocolate cake taste good mixed with gravy and salad dressing? No! Some foods need to be separate.

It is the same with computer programs. The computer stores programs in its **RAM**, or temporary, memory. If there is already a program in RAM, then your new program will get mixed up with the old one, just like your dinner and dessert.

NEW is a **command** that tells the computer to erase any program in its memory. Before entering a program, always type the letters *N E W* and press RETURN. Do it now!

Entering a BASIC Program

Now it is time to enter the first line of the BASIC program:

10 PRINT

Type the **number 1** then the **number 0**. (Be sure to use numbers, and not letters or you will have a **bug** in your program!) Next press the SPACE BAR. Then type the letters *P R I N T*.

Check this line for mistakes. If you find something wrong, back up and correct it. Press RETURN to put this step into the computer's RAM memory. Watch the cursor jump down to the next line on the screen. Enter the last four lines:

20 PRINT "THIS IS"
30 PRINT "MY FIRST"
40 PRINT "COMPUTER PROGRAM"
50 END

Did you remember to begin each line with its line number and end each line by pressing RETURN?

Running a Program

You have now entered a BASIC program. When you want the computer to do these steps, you use the BASIC command **RUN**. Type the letters *R U N* and press RETURN. You should see a blank line on the screen followed by

> THIS IS
> MY FIRST
> COMPUTER PROGRAM

If your BASIC program worked, give yourself a pat on the back. By typing RUN again, you can make the computer run your program once more. One nice thing about computers is that they never get bored. You can run your program as many times as you like.

Listing a Program

If your program did not work the first time, then you have some debugging to do. **Debugging** is taking a close look at your program and fixing any mistakes you find. Even if you cannot see your program on the screen, it *is* in the computer's memory. It will stay there until you type NEW, enter another program, or turn off the computer. To see your program, type *L I S T* and press RETURN. The **LIST** command tells the computer to take the program in memory and show its steps on the screen.

Making Corrections

After typing LIST, look carefully at the program steps. Can you find an error? If so, you can fix it. To correct a mistake in a line, simply retype the entire line.

Let's say you want to change the word *MY* in line 30 to your name. Retype the line, beginning with the number 30. But this time, instead of the word *MY*, type your name with an apostrophe *S* (*'S*) on the end. Do you see that line 30 is out of order on the screen? This does not bother the computer. Type RUN to see what happens. Try typing LIST, too.

Some Things to Try

PRINTING NUMBERS AND STRINGS: The PRINT statement gets the computer to show things on the screen. With computers, there is a difference between printing numbers and printing letters. You do not need quotation marks to print numbers. The computer will work just like a calculator. Type each line below, press RETURN, and see what happens:

```
PRINT 3
PRINT 5+2
PRINT 6-1
```

(Notice that these PRINT statements are not part of a program. You can use PRINT without a line number. If you do, the computer acts immediately after you press RETURN.)

You must warn the computer if you want it to print something other than a number. To print words or symbols you use quotation marks " " around them. These say, "WATCH OUT! HERE COMES A *STRING* OF LETTERS OR SYMBOLS." Type each line and then press RETURN:

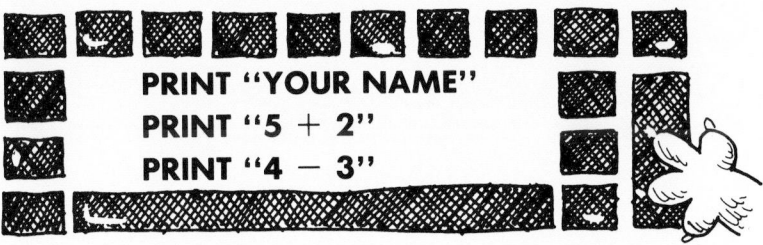

```
PRINT "YOUR NAME"
PRINT "5 + 2"
PRINT "4 - 3"
```

(Try an experiment. Type each of the three lines above but leave off the quotation marks. What happens?)

FUN WITH PRINT: Make up your own programs using PRINT. Before entering a program, remember to type NEW.

1. Write a program that prints a list of your favorite TV shows.

2. Write a program that prints the names of your family members.

3. Add lines to your family program so that each person's birth date shows up, too.

4. Play around with PRINT and you will find you can use it to draw designs. For example, try this tree design:

```
10 PRINT    "  X  "
20 PRINT    " XXX "
30 PRINT    "XXXXX"
40 PRINT    "  U  "
50 END
```

5. Can you use PRINT in a program to make a design of your own?

Using a Disk Drive or Cassette

When you turn off the computer, the program is erased from the RAM memory. But what if you want to save a program? Your computer has a command to permanently **SAVE** a program on a disk or cassette. Another command will find a program that has been saved, and **LOAD** it in the computer's memory.

Learn what your computer's special SAVE and LOAD commands are. Then practice using them.

Numbers and Your Computer

Computers are good at storing numbers and finding them again when needed. How do they do this? Imagine keeping your toys in boxes—each kind in a different box. This will help you understand how the computer stores numbers. To find

toys easily, you could label the boxes. In the box marked A, you might keep animals. Blocks could go in Box B, and cars in a box marked CARS. It does not matter how you label the boxes as long as you know what goes where. You can even change what is in the box without changing its label.

This same idea is used for storing numbers in a computer's memory. Each number is stored in a different location of the computer's memory. You choose a name or label for each storage location, just as you label the toy boxes. The labels can be letters like A and B, or X1 and K22. Sometimes they can even be short words. These labels are called **variables**.

A BASIC Program with Variables

Here is a BASIC program that uses variables:

```
5 LET A=2
10 LET B=3
15 LET C=A+B
20 PRINT C
25 END
```

In line 5, the BASIC statement, **LET A=2**, tells the computer to store the number 2 in a memory location labeled A. What number is stored at B? At C? Before trying this program, do the next activity.

Something to Do

A PENNY COMPUTER: Get three paper cups, a pencil, some paper, and ten pennies. Pretend the cups are memory locations in your computer. You are going to do the program listed above on your penny computer.

Look at line 5. **LET A=2** tells you to take a cup and label it with the letter A. When your cup is labeled, you put two pennies inside it. Now you have done the first step.

Line 10 of the program says **LET B=3**. That means you must label another cup with the letter B and then put three pennies in it. Next, look at line 15. **LET C=A+B** says to label another memory location with the letter C. Cup C is to hold an amount equal to A plus B. Look in cup A and see how many pennies it has. Leave the pennies in cup A and put the same number of pennies (two) into cup C. Then look in cup B and see how many pennies it has. Put that number of pennies (three) into cup C also.

The last line of the program says **PRINT C**. Look into cup C and count the pennies. Write that number on a piece of paper. Pretend the paper is your computer screen. What number did you write? Was it a 5?

Running the Addition Program

After trying the program with your penny computer, try it with your real computer. First, type NEW to clear the memory. Then type the five program lines, beginning each with its line number. Finish each line by pressing RETURN. What happens when you run the program? If there are no bugs, the computer will print a 5 on the screen.

Adding Other Numbers

A program that will add only 3 plus 2 is not very useful. What if you want to add different numbers? You would have to change the program. Let's say you want to add 4 plus 6. Change line 5 to **LET A = 4**. Line 10 should say **LET B = 6**. Type these new lines. List and run the program. How would you like to have to do this for each pair of numbers you want to add? An easier way is to use **INPUT**. Do the next activity to see how INPUT works.

Something to Do

PENNY POWER: Use the penny computer cups A, B, and C from the last activity. You also need about twenty pennies, a pencil, a piece of paper, and a friend to help you.

Your friend gets to choose two numbers to add on the penny computer. The first step is **INPUT A**. Have your friend put the first number of pennies in cup **A**. The next step, **INPUT B**, means your friend should put the second amount of pennies in cup B.

You do the third step, **LET C=A+B**. This means to put in cup C the number of pennies equal to A+B. To do this, you look in cup A and count the pennies, but don't take them out. Put that same number of pennies in cup C. Look in cup B and count those pennies. Put that number of pennies in cup C also. Now have the computer **PRINT C.** Look in cup C and count all the pennies. Write that number on paper, pretending it is the computer screen. Show it to your friend.

Can you see how this program is more powerful than the last one? You can use it over and over, for any two numbers your friend wants to input.

Using Input

Here is how the addition program looks using INPUT:

```
5 INPUT A
10 INPUT B
15 LET C=A+B
20 PRINT C
25 END
```

If the last program is still in your computer, do not type NEW. Simply retype lines 5 and 10. Leave lines 15, 20, and 25 alone and they will stay the same. LIST the program to check it. RUN the program and watch what happens. A question mark on the screen means the computer is waiting for your input. When you type a number and press RETURN, the computer stores your number in memory location A. Then it stops again with a question mark, waiting for you to input a number for B. Finally, it tells you the answer it gets when it adds your two numbers.

Some Things to Try

HELP! When the computer stops in the last program to wait for input, *you* know what to do but someone else might not. Try adding these three helping lines to the program:

> **3 PRINT "TYPE A NUMBER"**
> **7 PRINT "TYPE ANOTHER NUMBER"**
> **18 PRINT "THE SUM IS ";**

LIST the program to see how it looks. RUN the program. Try it on a friend. It should now make sense to anyone who uses it. This is the kind of work computer programmers go through to make a program better.

Do you know what the semicolon symbol ; in line 18 does? Type line 18 without the semicolon. Run the program again. What happens?

FUN WITH BASIC: Making changes to a program is a good way to learn more about BASIC. Try changing the addition program into a subtraction program. What kind of problems might you have with this program? (HINT: Before the second input, type this line: **7 PRINT "TYPE A SMALLER NUMBER"** .)

Round and Round with BASIC

The programs you have seen so far have been simple ones. The computer followed them straight through from beginning to end. But what about all the marvelous things people do with computer programs—sending satellites into orbit, creating exciting games, and making short work of tedious office jobs?

Learning about loops will give you more computer power. A **loop** is a part of a computer program which is repeated. There are several ways to make loops in BASIC programs. Here you will learn one of them.

To have the computer print your name ten times, you *could* write a program with ten print statements. But a shorter way is to make a loop with **FOR** and **NEXT**. FOR marks the beginning of a loop. NEXT shows where the loop ends. On the line with FOR, you use a **counter**. The counter is a variable that tells the computer how many times to repeat the loop.

Type NEW to clear the memory. Then enter and run this BASIC program on your computer. See if you can figure out how the FOR/NEXT loop works before doing the next activity.

```
5 FOR T=1 TO 10
10 PRINT "YOUR NAME"
15 NEXT T
20 END
```

Something to Do

PENNY LOOPS: A penny computer can help you understand FOR and NEXT in the program above. You need a pencil, paper, eleven pennies, and a cup labeled *T.* Cup T counts the times you have gone through the loop.

Start with cup T empty. Line 5 tells you to set your counter T at 1. Do this by putting one penny in T. Line 10 has you print your name on the paper. In line 15, **NEXT T** tells you to go back up to line 5. Put another penny in cup T. Now your counter is set at 2. Move down to line 10 and print your name on the paper again.

Keep going around the loop, repeating these steps. When there are ten pennies in T, print your name for the tenth time. Then line 15 sends you back up to line 5 once more. This time, when you put a penny in T, it makes eleven pennies. But line 5 says T can count from 1 to 10. When T goes past 10, you get "kicked out" of the loop. You move down to the line after the NEXT statement and continue with the program. In this case, that line says END, so your program is done.

COUNTING: FOR/NEXT can also be used for counting. Type NEW, then enter and run this program.

> **5 PRINT "I CAN COUNT TO FIVE"**
> **10 FOR N=1 TO 5**
> **15 PRINT N**
> **20 NEXT N**
> **25 END**

Notice that the counting variable here is labeled N. Use a penny computer to figure out how this program works. You will see that it counts the number of pennies in the cup.

EXPERIMENTING WITH FOR/NEXT: Change lines 5 and 10 so that the program above counts to 20. Next, try to write a program that counts from 10 to 20.

Looking at BASIC

You are getting to know your computer by learning to speak its language—BASIC. So far, you have entered and run several BASIC programs—some simple ones, some with loops. To do fancier programs, you will need to know even more about BASIC.

But remember, you are learning a new language. Practice with the BASIC words you know. Start by making small changes to a program. Then try writing simple programs of your own. Take your time and learn a little each day. The more you practice, the easier it will be for you to talk to your computer.

Find Out More About BASIC

READ BOOKS ABOUT BASIC. Look in bookstores, computer stores, software stores, and libraries for books on BASIC. Here are three books you might start with:

Computers For Kids, by Sally Greenwood Larsen, Creative Computing Press, 1981. Find the version of this book that matches the brand of computer you use. It tells about flowcharting and simple BASIC programming.

Basic Beginnings, by Susan Drake Lipscomb and Margaret Ann Zuanich, Avon/Camelot Books, 1983. This book gives you simple BASIC programs to enter and run, plus suggestions for changes you can make.

Fun with Microcomputers and BASIC, by Donald D. Spencer, Reston Publishing Company, 1981. The second half of this book gives problems to solve as well as BASIC programs for you to enter and run on your computer.

You can find many other books with programs to enter and run on your computer. Look for ones with short programs that are no more than a page long.

JOIN A COMPUTER CLUB OR GO TO COMPUTER CAMP. A club or a camp is a fun way to learn more about BASIC. To find out what is offered, ask your teacher, librarian, or computer specialist. And be sure to say that you are interested in BASIC!

Words About Computers

BASIC. A popular programming language for computers.
Bug. A mistake in a computer program.
Command. A BASIC word, such as NEW, LIST, and RUN, which deals with a whole program.
END. The last statement used in a BASIC program.
FOR/NEXT. The BASIC words used to make a loop.
INPUT. A BASIC statement which lets enter a number.
LET. A BASIC statement which gives a label to one of the computer's memory locations.
Line number. The number in front of a program line.
LIST. The BASIC command to show a program's steps on the screen.
LOAD. The BASIC command which sends a program from the disk to the computer's memory.
Loop. A part of a computer program which is repeated.
NEW. The command to clear the computer's memory.
PRINT. The BASIC statement which tells the computer to print something on the screen.
Program. Instructions that tell a computer what to do.
Programming language. The set of rules, symbols, and words you use for writing a computer program.
RAM. (Random Access Memory). The computer's temporary memory where a program is stored.
RUN. The command which tells the computer to carry out the program in memory.
SAVE. The BASIC command that sends a program from the computer's temporary memory onto a disk for permanent storage.
Statement. A word used in a program which the computer understands and obeys. PRINT and END are BASIC statements.
Variable. A label given to a computer's memory location.

Index

Addition program, 20–25

BASIC, 5
Bugs, 13

Cassette, 19
Commands
 LIST, 15
 NEW, 12
 RUN, 14
Computer, penny, 21, 23, 27
Corrections, making, 16
Counter, 26
Counting, 28
Cursor, 7
Cursor-moving keys, 7

Debugging, 15
Directions, 4
Disk, 19

END statement, 8, 11
Erasing a program, 12, 19

FOR/NEXT loops, 26–28

INPUT, 22, 24

Keyboard, 4, 6, 7

Language, 4, 5
Line numbers, 8, 10
LIST command, 15

LOAD program, 19
Loops, 26

Memory, 12, 19
Mistakes, correcting, 15, 16

NEW, 12
Numbers, storing, 19–20

Penny computer, 21, 23, 27
Penny loops, 27
PRINT statement, 8, 17
Programming languages, 5

Quotation marks, use of in BASIC, 11

RAM, 12, 19
Return, 7
RUN, 14

SAVE program, 19. *See also* Memory.
Shift, 7
Simple program, 8
Space bar, 7
Statements, 11
 END, 8, 11
 PRINT, 8, 11, 17, 18
Storage, number, 19–20

"Talking" to a computer, 4

Variables, 20